IRISH COOKING

CLB 2626
© 1991 Colour Library Books Ltd, Godalming, Surrey, England.
All rights reserved.
This 1991 edition published by Crescent Books,
distributed by Outlet Book Company, Inc, a Random House Company,
225 Park Avenue South, New York, New York 10003.
Printed and bound in Singapore
ISBN 0 517 05919 3
8 7 6 5 4 3 2 1

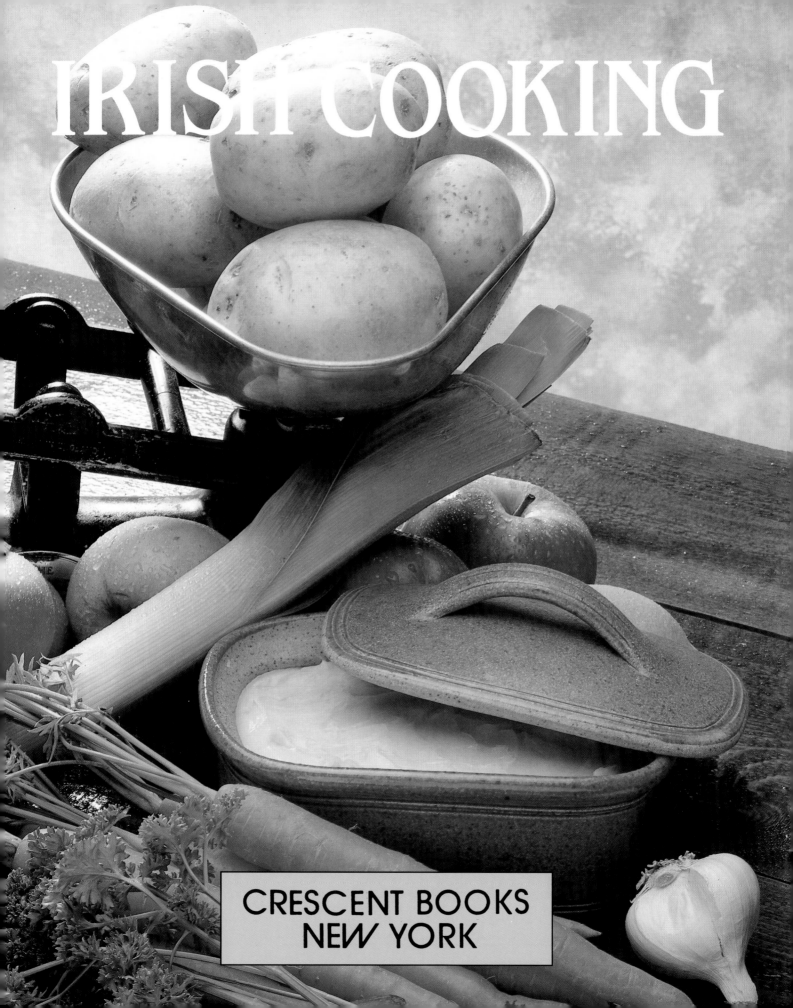

IRISH COOKING

CRESCENT BOOKS
NEW YORK

INTRODUCTION

The Irish are renowned throughout the world for the friendliness and hospitality they show to guests, whether friends or strangers. Such has been the case since pagan times, when even kings and princes were governed by the Brehon Laws – very precise rules about hospitality and etiquette that were originally formulated in the fifth century. One person the royal court was always eager to take particular care of was the court poet, or the visiting man of letters. Then, as now, the Irish venerated their poets and literary men, and were mortally afraid of offending them lest they be satirized as a result. In the *Book of Ballymote*, for example, a poet writes of his host's lack of hospitality: "Shall salt be sprinkled on your food? asked the servant. No, said he, for there is nothing to sprinkle it on, unless it is my tongue, but that is not necessary as it is bitter enough already."

In the days of the Brehon Laws, the wealth of kings was reckoned according to the number of cattle in their herds. Young bulls were slaughtered for veal, and meat was salted down for winter use. Sheep were plentiful in the uplands and herds of swine fed on acorns in the oak forests; wild boar, deer, and huge Irish hares abounded, while the skies were full of game birds. The Vikings taught the native Irish the art of preserving food, such as dried, salted or smoked fish or meat, as well as the value of pickling various foods in vinegar.

Between 1962 and 1967, archaeologists discovered the site of the tenth-century Viking city of Dublin at Wood Quay in Dublin, together with much of the later medieval city. The remains in the rubbish pits proved that not only were beef, mutton and seafood all on the ancient Irish menu, but so too were desserts in the form of apples, strawberries, cherries, plums and hazelnuts. However, although the more sophisticated citizens dined on grapes and figs, the poor subsisted on gruel or porridge and weed or nettle soup.

In early Celtic society, the black or white blood puddings that are still served today were common fare. Butter was also in general use, and was often preserved in oak chests and buried in bogland for later use. Gull and goose eggs were plentiful, and seal or porpoise was often added to the plentiful supply of fish and seafood. Cereals in common use were wheat, barley, corn, oats and rye. Milk was used in vast quantities.

The potato, often associated with Ireland, was actually unknown in Ireland until it was introduced in Elizabethan times by Sir Walter Raleigh, when he was Mayor of Youghal, in County Cork. It soon became a staple food. The great potato famines of the 1840s and '50s were a man-made tragedy; Ireland was bursting with food, but the cereals and dairy produce were for export only and so the peasants starved in their millions when their staple food, the potato, failed in a series of disastrous harvests.

Visitors to Ireland could also rely on the hospitality of the monasteries. The monks lived frugally enough, but their guests enjoyed a life of plenty, partaking of fish, flesh and fowl. The monastic cooks used salt, pepper, mustard, ginger, olive oil, walnuts, figs, almonds and rice to enhance their dishes.

Many of the foods eaten in these early Irish societies are still popular today. Ireland has a great wealth of seafood, such as cockles and mussels, and its seas and rivers are still rich in fish. The country's lush farmland is ideal for raising the sheep and cattle that provide the variety of meat dishes that are very much a part of the everyday Irish diet.

Most importantly, today, as always, the tradition of hospitality continues in Ireland!

The rugged beauty of the Corca Dhuibhne Peninsula (right), in County Kerry, conceals a wealth of pre- and early historic remains.

Nettle Soup

Preparation Time: 15 minutes **Cooking Time:** 30 minutes **Serves:** 6-8

Nettle soup was part of the diet of the monks in Ireland as far back as the 6th century. It would often have been made with milk alone, or even milk and water, and you can vary the proportions of stock and milk used in this recipe.

Ingredients
2¹/₂ cups nettles
¹/₄ cup butter
¹/₃ cup fine oatmeal

3³/₄ cups stock
1¹/₄ cups milk

Wear gloves when you are collecting the nettles and only choose the young, bright green leaves. Remove any stalks and chop up the leaves. These days a food processor will do the job in a fraction of the time it takes to chop them by hand. Melt the butter in a large saucepan. Add the oatmeal and cook until the mixture is a golden brown. Remove the pan from the heat and add the stock. Bring it to the boil and add the milk. When it is boiling again, add the chopped nettles and cook for another few minutes. You may need more seasoning, depending how much seasoning there is in the stock.

The most outstanding features that remain of Cong Abbey, once home to 1,000 monks, are the three exquisite doorways in Early Gothic style.

Potato Soup

Preparation Time: 20 minutes **Cooking Time:** 1 hour 15 minutes **Serves:** 8-10

For best results, use a home-made stock. Boil down a chicken carcass with an onion, a carrot and some herbs. Strain off the stock and let it get cold. Remove any fat from the top and you will have a lovely, thick jelly which will keep for a week in the refrigerator or can be kept in the freezer for longer.

Ingredients
2lbs potatoes	2$\frac{1}{2}$ cups milk
2 onions	Bay leaf, parsley and thyme
1 small carrot	Salt and pepper
$\frac{1}{4}$ cup butter	Cream and chives for garnishing
5 cups stock	

Peel and slice the potatoes, onions and carrot. Melt butter in a large saucepan and sweat onions in it until soft but not brown. Add potatoes and carrot. Stir in the stock and milk. Tie the bay leaf, thyme and parsley together and add, along with pepper and salt to taste. Simmer gently for about an hour then either liquify or put through a sieve or vegetable mill. Add some cream before serving and sprinkle with chopped chives.

County Kerry is a quiet rural area which has close links with America – many emigrants left the west coast for the new land across the sea.

Smoked Salmon Bisque

Preparation Time: 30 minutes **Cooking Time:** 1 hour **Serves:** 6-8

A side of smoked salmon is a rare gift these days, the price being what it is. If you should be the lucky recipient of one, be sure to save the skin and trimmings as they will make a delicious soup.

Ingredients

Skin and trimmings of a side
    of smoked salmon
1 onion, stuck with cloves
1 carrot
1-2 sticks of celery
Bay leaf
1 tsp salt

Few peppercorns
$\frac{1}{4}$ cup butter
$\frac{1}{2}$ cup flour
1 tbsp tomato paste
1 glass white wine
4 tbsps cream and
1 tbsp parsley for garnishing

Put the skin and trimmings in a saucepan. Cut the carrot and celery into chunks. Pierce the onion with 5-6 cloves. Add these to the pan. Cover with cold water, add the bay leaf, salt and peppercorns. Cover the pan and simmer for about 30 minutes. Remove the bay leaf. Take out the onion, remove the cloves and return the onion to the pan. With a slotted spoon, remove the fish skin and scrape off any remaining flesh, which should also be returned to the pan. Strain half the liquid into a bowl.

In another large pan melt the butter, stir in the flour and make a roux. Stir in the tomato paste and gradually add the strained stock, stirring constantly until it thickens. Add a glass of white wine, or a glass of sherry will do very well! Put the rest of the stock, containing the fish and vegetables, in the liquidizer and run it for half a minute. Add this to the soup. Test for seasoning. You can either stir a spoonful of cream into the soup before serving or put a spoon of cream on top of each bowl. Garnish with a little chopped parsley.

With its abundance of trout, perch and pike, Ashleagh Falls near Leenane, in County Galway, is a haven for fishermen.

Mussels in White Wine

Preparation Time: 15 minutes **Cooking Time:** 30 minutes **Serves:** 3-4

Ingredients

60 mussels
1 large onion, finely chopped
½ bottle dry white wine
2 tsps flour

2 tsps butter
Salt and pepper
2 tbsps parsiey, chopped
Pinch of ground nutmeg

Wash the mussels well under cold, running water, scrubbing with a stiff brush. Discard any mussels that are open or those that have cracked shells. Place in a large saucepan and add the onion and wine. Cover and bring to the boil. Cook for about 5 minutes, or until all the mussels are open, shaking the saucepan from time to time. Strain the liquor into another saucepan. Remove the top shells and beards, and put the mussels into warmed soup plates; keep warm. Blend the flour into the butter and add to the strained liquor. Bring the mixture to the boil, stirring constantly as it thickens. Season to taste. Add the parsley and pour over the mussels.

A statue of Molly Malone and her barrow stands at the bottom of Grafton Street in Dublin.

Crubeens

Preparation Time: 5 minutes   **Cooking Time:** 3 hours

Ingredients

1 pig's trotter (foot) per person
1 onion
1 carrot
Pinch of salt

Few peppercorns
1 bay leaf
Chopped parsley and thyme

Put all the ingredients in a pan, cover with cold water, bring to the boil and simmer for three hours. Serve surrounded by lettuce and with a tomato garnish.

The Long Hall is an atmospheric old Dublin bar – perfect for relaxing with a pint of Guinness or an Irish whiskey!

Drisheen

Preparation Time: 40 minutes **Cooking Time:** 45 minutes **Serves:** 8

Drisheen is a white pudding which is only found in County Cork. It is made from sheep's blood mixed with salt, cream, oatmeal or breadcrumbs and seasoned with mace and tansy. It can be bought ready-made in Cork and in Dublin in the shape of thick sausages, but the home-made sort was usually made in a wide, shallow pan and steamed or baked in the oven in a bain marie.

Ingredients
4 cups sheep's blood
2 tsps salt
2¹/₂ cups creamy milk

Pinch tansy or thyme
2 cups breadcrumbs

Strain the blood into a mixing bowl, add all the other ingredients and mix well. Allow to stand for half an hour, then pour mixture into a greased ovenproof dish. Cover with foil and place in a roasting pan with enough water to come halfway up the sides of the dish. Bake in the oven at 350°F for 45 minutes or until set. Serve garnished with lettuce and tomato.

Cork, the third largest city in Ireland, is beautifully situated on the River Lee.

Colcannon

Preparation Time: 10 minutes **Cooking Time:** 20 minutes **Serves:** 4

Colcannon is a traditional potato dish that is associated with Hallowe'en. It is a mixture of cabbage or kale and mashed potato which sometimes has leeks or green onions mixed in.

Ingredients

¹/₂ cup finely chopped onion, leek or scallion	¹/₄ cup creamy milk
¹/₄ cup butter	1lb cooked mashed potatoes
	1¹/₂ cups cooked cabbage

Gently fry the onion in melted butter until soft. Add the milk and the well-mashed potatoes and stir until heated through. Chop the cabbage finely and beat into the mixture over a low heat until all the mixture is pale green and fluffy. This dish is an excellent accompaniment for boiled ham.

The Giant's Causeway is the result of ancient volcanic activity, although legend has it that the basalt columns were the stepping stones of the famed giant Fionn MacCool.

Boxty Pancakes

Preparation Time: 20 minutes **Cooking Time:** 15 minutes **Serves:** 6

These are made with a mixture of cooked and raw potatoes, combined with flour and bound with potato starch and fat. Milk or buttermilk is added to make the mixture into a dropping consistency and the pancakes are cooked on a griddle.

Ingredients

¹/₂lb raw potatoes	2 cups flour
8oz mashed potatoes	Pepper
1 tsp salt	¹/₄ cup butter, margarine or bacon fat
1 tsp baking soda	Milk

Peel and grate the raw potatoes. Wrap them tightly in a cloth and squeeze over a bowl to extract as much of the starch liquid as possible. Thoroughly blend the grated raw potato into the cooked mashed potato. Pour the liquid off the bowl of potato starch and scrape the starch into the potato mixture. Sift the salt and baking soda with the flour and add to the potatoes, mix well. Add the melted fat and mix again. Add as much milk as necessary to make the mixture into a batter of dropping consistency, season with pepper and cook in spoonfuls on a greased griddle or heavy pan until crispy and golden on both sides.

During the summer months the tree-lined Grand Canal in Dublin is a popular waterway for boating.

Poached Salmon Garni

Preparation Time: 2-3 hours **Cooking Time:** 20-30 minutes **Serves:** 8-10

Here is a simple way to cook and serve fresh salmon without the need for a fish kettle.

Ingredients

1 fresh salmon, approx 2½lbs, cleaned, with head removed
1 tbsp vinegar
1 large lettuce
5-6 hard-cooked eggs, quartered
1 lemon, sliced
1 cucumber, sliced
3-4 firm tomatoes, sliced
Mayonnaise for garnish
Dill for garnish

Cut the fish in two, near the gills. Place each piece on a well-buttered piece of foil and make a parcel, folding the join several times and folding in the ends. Place the two pieces in a saucepan large enough to hold them side by side, cover them with cold water, add the vinegar and bring slowly to the boil. Gently turn the parcels over in the water. Turn off the heat, cover the pot and leave to cool. Before the fish is completely cold put the parcels on a large plate, unwrap them and carefully skin and bone the fish. Divide each section into serving-size pieces along the grain of the fish.

Lay the salmon portions in two rows, the length of one or two serving platters, with lettuce leaves between them. Slice the hard-cooked eggs and arrange slices overlapping.

Allow a slice of lemon for each salmon portion and place accordingly. Slice the cucumber and tomatoes and arrange together on the platter. Garnish the salmon with sprigs of dill and serve the mayonnaise separately.

The peace and tranquility of Connemara makes it one of Ireland's most popular tourist attractions.

Dublin Bay Prawn Cocktail

Preparation Time: 15 minutes   **Serves:** 4

Dublin Bay Shrimps are very large and rather expensive, so for shrimp cocktail it is better to use ordinary shrimp and garnish the cocktail with king shrimp.

Ingredients
5-6 lettuce leaves

½lb cooked, shelled shrimp
(frozen shrimp will do)

A little chopped parsley

4 jumbo shrimp

4 lemon wedges

Cocktail sauce
4 heaping tbsps mayonnaise

2 tbsps tomato paste

1 tsp Worcestershire sauce

2 tsps lemon juice

4 tsps medium sherry

2 tbsps whipped cream

To make the sauce, add the paste, Worcestershire sauce, lemon juice and sherry to the mayonnaise and mix well. Fold in the whipped cream. Shred the lettuce finely and divide between four glass goblets. If using frozen shrimp, drain them well and place equal amounts on top of the lettuce. Just before serving, coat the shrimp with the cocktail sauce and sprinkle a pinch of the chopped parsley on top of each. Garnish with a jumbo shrimp and a lemon wedge on each glass. Serve with buttered brown soda bread.

Dublin takes its name from the Irish *Dubh Linn* meaning "dark pool," which refers to the River Liffey as it runs through the heart of the city.

Salmon Flan

Preparation Time: 10 minutes **Cooking Time:** 40-45 minutes **Serves:** 4-6

This would make an excellent luncheon or supper dish for four people. Serve it either with a salad and brown bread and butter or with baked potatoes and petit pois.

Ingredients
6oz frozen puff paste
2 tsps cornstarch
$^2/_3$ cup milk
Salt and pepper

6oz cooked fresh salmon or
    7$^1/_2$oz can of salmon
1 egg, lightly beaten
Dill for garnish

Thaw the pastry. Roll out into a square large enough to line a greased 8-inch quiche pan. Trim off the excess pastry and crimp the edges. Mix the cornstarch with 1 tbsp of the milk, bring the rest to the boil, pour into the cornstarch mix, stir well and return to the pan. Return to the boil and cook for 1 minute, stirring constantly. Season well with salt and pepper. If using canned salmon drain the liquid from the can into the sauce. If using fresh salmon add 1 tbsp of butter. Remove the pan from the heat and add the egg, beating it in thoroughly. Flake up the salmon, removing any bones and skin, fold it into the sauce and turn into the pie shell. Bake in the oven, 375°F, for 35-40 minutes. Serve garnished with dill sprigs.

The area around the River Blackwater in County Meath is renowned for its hunting and fishing.

Baked Stuffed Mackerel

Preparation Time: 15 minutes **Cooking Time:** 30 minutes **Serves:** 4

Mackerel should be eaten the day it is caught so this is a recipe for people living near the ocean.

Ingredients

1 small onion, finely chopped
¼ cup butter
1 tbsp oatmeal
2 cups breadcrumbs
4 mackerel, well cleaned and washed
1 heaping tsp fresh chopped
    lemon thyme

1 heaping tsp fresh chopped
    parsley or ½ tsp of each, dried
Salt and pepper
2-3 tbsps hot water
1 lemon

Fry the chopped onion in the butter to soften. Add the oatmeal, breadcrumbs, herbs and seasoning. Mix well. Bind with the hot water. Fill the cavities of the fish with the stuffing and wrap each one separately in well-buttered foil. Place in a roasting pan or on a cookie sheet and bake in a pre-heated oven at 375°F, for 25-30 minutes. Serve with lemon slices and extra lemon thyme.

With its miles of sandy beaches and beautiful clear waters the area around Tramore is a popular spot with both tourists and locals.

Grilled Trout with Almonds

Preparation Time: 10 minutes **Cooking Time:** 15 minutes **Serves:** 4

Ingredients

4 fresh trout
1 lemon, quartered
¼ cup butter

¼ cup slivered almonds
Parsley for garnish

Clean the trout. Place a lemon wedge in the cavity of each. Line the broiler pan with buttered foil and carefully lay the fish on it. Smear a little butter on each. Preheat the broiler and cook the trout under it for 5 minutes. Turn them very carefully, put a little more butter on top and broil for another five minutes. Keep the fish warm on plates while you toss the almonds in the butter in the broiler pan and brown them under the broiler. Sprinkle them over the fish. Serve with a garnish of lemon slices and parsley.

The magnificent state apartments in Dublin Castle have been the subject of extensive restoration work, but little now remains of the castle's medieval origins.

Sole Surprise

Preparation Time: 30 minutes **Cooking Time:** 30 minutes **Serves:** 4

This recipe consists of little puff paste "boxes" filled with spinach, with the fillets of sole laid on top and coated with a cheese sauce.

Ingredients
8oz frozen puff paste

8oz frozen spinach

1/4 cup butter

4 small or 2 large fillets of sole

Sauce
2 tbsps butter

2 tbsps flour

1 1/4 cups milk

Pinch of fennel

Salt and pepper

1/2 cup grated cheese

Roll out the defrosted pastry into a rectangle 5x8 inches. Cut into four equal size rectangles 2 1/2 x4 inches. Follow the same procedure for each one. Fold the dough over, short sides together. Cut out the center with a sharp knife, leaving 1/2 inch all round. Roll out the center piece on a floured board until it is the same size as the 1/2 inch "frame". Brush the edges with milk and put the "frame" on the base. Brush the top with milk and place on a greased cookie sheet. Bake the pastry in the oven, 425°F, for 10-15 minutes.

Meanwhile, put the spinach in a pan with 1/4 inch water and a little salt. Cover and cook for 4-5 minutes. Drain and beat in half the butter. Skin the fillets and, if necessary, cut them in two. Use the rest of the butter to coat two plates and put the fillets on one and cover them with the other. Cook them over a pan of boiling water for twenty minutes.

For the sauce, melt the 2 tbsps butter with the flour to make a roux. Gradually stir in the milk. Bring to the boil. Reduce heat and add fennel and salt and pepper; cook for another minute or two. Remove from the heat and stir in the grated cheese.

Divide the spinach between the four pastry boxes. Lay the sole on top and top the fish with the cheese sauce.

Castle Island is just one of the islands located on Lough Key, which itself forms part of the River Shannon system of lakes in County Roscommon.

Pheasant Braised in Red Wine

Preparation Time: 15 minutes **Cooking Time:** 1 hour 15 minutes **Serves:** 4

Ingredients

2 tbsps oil
1 tbsp butter
1 large pheasant, dressed
2 eating apples
1 onion
4 tsps flour
$\frac{2}{3}$ cup stock or water

$\frac{2}{3}$ cup red wine
Rind and juice of 1 orange
1 heaping tsp brown sugar
Salt and pepper
Bay leaf, sprig of parsley and thyme,
    tied together

Preheat the oven to 350°F. Melt the oil and butter in a heavy pan. Add the pheasant, turning it to brown all over, then remove and place it in a casserole with the apples. Chop the onion and add it to the fat in the pan. Allow it to soften without browning. Stir in the flour then gradually add the stock and the wine and bring to the boil, stirring constantly. Add the grated orange rind, the orange juice and the sugar. Season with pepper and pour the sauce over the pheasant. Add the herbs, cover the casserole and bake in the preheated oven for one hour.

The rolling countryside around Knocknanash, County Waterford.

Limerick Ham

Preparation Time: 12 hours

Limerick ham was smoked using a special recipe in which juniper berries were added to the fire to produce the distinctive flavor. It has been famous all over the world since the 18th century.

Ingredients

1 smoked ham
1 clove-studded onion
Few peppercorns

1 tbsp honey or brown sugar
Browned breadcrumbs, optional

Soak the ham in water for at least twelve hours, rinse and cover with cold water. Add the clove-studded onion, peppercorns and honey. Bring slowly to the boil, skim, then simmer for 20 minutes to the pound plus 20 additional minutes. The ham is cooked when the thick skin peels back easily. Remove the ham from the water and peel off the skin. If it is to be served hot, coat the ham with browned breadcrumbs and place it in a roasting pan in the oven, 350°F, for 40 minutes. If it is to be eaten cold it should be replaced in the pot after the skin has been removed and allowed to cool in the liquor in which it was cooked. To glaze, heat equal amounts of brown sugar, vinegar and apricot jam, stirring until melted, and then pour the mixture over the ham.

The site of this traditional thatched cottage in Connemara was obviously carefully chosen – near fresh water and in a sheltered position.

Beef Braised in Guinness

Preparation Time: 15 minutes **Cooking Time:** 1 hour 45 minutes **Serves:** 4

Ingredients

1¹/₂lbs chuck or round steak
2 medium onions
¹/₂lb carrots
2 heaping tbsps flour
Salt and pepper

2-3 tbsps cooking oil
¹/₂ tsp fresh basil, minced
²/₃ cup Guinness ale
1 tsp honey
²/₃ cup stock or water

The steak should be about 1-inch (2.5cm) thick and cut into about twelve pieces.

Peel the onions and chop them fairly small. Peel the carrots and slice them into pieces about the size of your little finger. Place the flour in a flat dish and mix in a tsp of salt and a good sprinkling of pepper. Heat the oil in the pan, add the onions and cook until soft. Transfer them with a slotted spoon to a large, shallow, greased, ovenproof dish. Dip the pieces of meat in the seasoned flour and brown them in the fat in the pan. Remove these as they are cooked and place in the dish on top of the onions, in a single layer. Arrange the carrots around them. If necessary, add a little more oil to the pan and stir in the remainder of the seasoned flour. Cook for a minute or two, stirring constantly, then add the basil and the Guinness. Allow to boil for a minute or two add the honey and the stock. Return to the boil and pour over the meat. Cover the dish either with a lid or with foil and cook in the oven at 325°F for 1¹/₂ hours. This dish tastes even better if you cook it the day before and heat it up again in the oven for about 45 minutes. If the gravy looks as though it needs thickening, mix 1 tsp of arrowroot with 2 tbsps of cold water and stir into the gravy 15 minutes before the cooking time is up.

Ireland's mild, damp climate and the country's sparse population mean that farming is still the biggest employer in most rural areas.

Stuffed Breast of Lamb

Preparation Time: 15 minutes **Cooking Time:** 1 hour 30 minutes **Serves:** 4

Ingredients
Half breast of lamb
1 medium onion
Salt and pepper
4 cups white breadcrumbs
¼ cup chopped suet

½ tsp marjoram
½ tsp thyme
Grated rind of half a lemon
1 egg
1 tbsp flour

Bone the breast of lamb with a sharp knife. Place the bones in a saucepan with half the onion and some salt and pepper. Cover them with water, bring to the boil, skim, cover the pot and simmer for half an hour.

Mix the breadcrumbs, suet, herbs, lemon rind, a little salt and pepper and the other half of the onion, minced, and bind them with the egg. Add 2-3 tbsps of the bone stock and spread the stuffing on the breast of lamb. Roll up, starting at the wide end. Tie up firmly with string and place in a greased roasting pan. Bake in the oven, 400°F, for 1 hour.

Transfer the meat to a serving dish and keep hot while you make the gravy. Drain off any excess fat from the roasting pan, retaining about two tbsps. Stir in the flour and heat on the stove until mixture browns. Stir in about a cupful of the stock. Bring to the boil, stirring constantly. Boil for a few minutes and then strain into a gravy boat and serve with the stuffed lamb. Serve with new potatoes and zucchini.

One of the best ways to see Ireland is to stay at one of the many farmhouses which offer accommodation and a warm welcome to visitors.

Cold Chicken in Tarragon Sauce

Preparation Time: 45 minutes **Cooking Time:** 1 hour 20 minutes **Serves:** 6-8

This recipe is ideal for a summer lunch or supper party as it can be prepared well in advance. Serve with new potatoes and a salad or with rice mixed with vegetables.

Ingredients

3½lb chicken with feet
   and giblets
Salt and pepper
Tarragon

1 onion, quartered
1 carrot, quartered
1 stick celery, quartered
1 bay leaf

Sauce

¼ cup butter
½ cup flour
Glass white wine or cider
1 tsp chopped tarragon

2 tsps chopped parsley
Juice of ½ lemon
3 heaping tbsps whipped cream
3 heaping tbsps mayonnaise

Generously sprinkle the inside of the chicken with salt, pepper and tarragon. Place the onion, carrot and celery in a saucepan just large enough to hold the chicken snugly. Add giblets and chicken feet. Place the chicken on top and pour over enough water just to cover. Cover the pan tightly and bring to the boil. Reduce heat and simmer for 1 hour. Remove the pan from the heat and carefully turn the chicken breast-side down in the stock, taking care not to break the skin. Cover again and allow to cool. This can be done the day before. Skin the chicken and remove all the flesh from the bones, slicing the meat from the legs into longish slivers and dividing the white parts up into similar-sized pieces.

Melt the butter in a heavy saucepan. Stir in the flour and cook for a minute or two. Add the white wine. Gradually stir in the 1¼ cups of stock. Add the tarragon, parsley and lemon juice and bring the sauce to the boil. Cook for a further 2 minutes, stirring constantly. Remove from the heat and allow to cool slightly before folding in the whipped cream and finally, the mayonnaise. Toss the chicken pieces in about ¾ of the sauce and pile them into a large, shallow serving dish. Coat with the remainder of the sauce and garnish with tarragon sprigs and strips of lemon rind before serving.

Irish Stew

Preparation Time: 30 minutes **Cooking Time:** 2-2½ hours **Serves:** 4

Either boned mutton, cut up and with most of the fat removed, or best end of rib chops, trimmed but left on the bone, can be used for this dish. The most important points to remember are not to use too much liquid in the cooking and to cook the stew very slowly so that it doesn't dry out.

Ingredients

2lbs boned mutton or
   3lbs rib chops
2lbs potatoes
2 large onions
Salt and pepper

1 tbsp fresh, chopped thyme
   and parsley or 1 tsp dried thyme
1½ cups water
Chopped parsley for garnish

Trim the meat, leaving a little of the fat on. Peel and slice the potatoes and onions. Season the meat and vegetables with salt, pepper and herbs. Then, starting and finishing with a layer of potatoes, layer the potatoes, meats and onions in a large saucepan or casserole. Add the water and cover tightly. Either simmer on a very low heat on the top of the stove for 2-2½ hours or cook in a slow oven, 275°F for the same length of time. The pot or casserole should be shaken occasionally to prevent the potatoes from sticking and you should check that the liquid has not dried out. The finished stew should not be too runny and the potatoes should thicken it sufficiently. Brown the top potato layer under a hot broiler and serve sprinkled with chopped parsley.

Bringing home the hay in the Gap of Mamore, County Donegal.

Boiled Ham and Cabbage

Preparation Time: 2-3 hours **Cooking Time:** 1 hour 45 minutes **Serves:** 6-8

Ingredients
Piece of uncooked ham about 3lbs in weight
1¹/₂-2lbs green cabbage
¹/₂ medium-sized onion or one small onion cut in two

Parsley Sauce
1¹/₄ cups stock
¹/₄ cup butter or margarine
3 tbsps flour

1¹/₄ cups milk
¹/₂ cup chopped parsley

Soak the ham for several hours or cover it with cold water, bring to the boil, discard water and cover meat with more boiling water. Bring it back to the boil, skim and simmer for 20 minutes to the pound and 20 minutes over. Reserve the stock.

Meanwhile, cut the cabbage in two and cut out a V in the stalk end of both halves to remove the fiberous end of the stalk. Cut the two halves down through the V and rinse the quarters in salted water. Place in a large saucepan with the cut onion (this miraculously seems to prevent the usual smell of cooked cabbage permeating the house). When the ham is cooked add 3-4 ladles of the stock to the cabbage, cover tightly and cook for about 20 minutes. Meanwhile, skin the ham, cut a lattice pattern in the fat, coat it with brown sugar and stud it with cloves. Brown it in a hot oven while the cabbage is cooking. Drain the cabbage and remove the onion.

Measure out 1¹/₄ cups of the stock in which the cabbage was cooked to use for the parsley sauce. Melt butter or margarine in a saucepan, stir in the flour and make a roux. Cook without browning for a minute or two. Gradually add the stock and then the milk. Bring to the boil and stir for a few minutes. Add the chopped parsley. Adjust the seasoning. Serve with the ham and cabbage and potatoes boiled in their jackets.

Westport Bay near Murrisk, County Mayo epitomizes the peace and tranquillity which are so much a part of rural life in Ireland.

Marinated Pork Chops

Preparation Time: 3-4 hours **Cooking Time:** 1 hour **Serves:** 4

Ingredients

4 pork chops
1 onion, finely chopped
$^1/_2$ tsp sage
$^1/_2$ tsp thyme
1 cup cider
2 tbsps oil
1 tbsp butter

$^1/_2$ cup flour, seasoned
   with salt and pepper
1 or 2 apples, peeled, cored and sliced
$^3/_4$ cup stock
1 tsp honey
1 tsp French mustard

Place the chops in a shallow ovenproof dish just large enough to hold them. Add the onion and herbs to the cider and pour over the chops. Leave for several hours, turning the meat occasionally. Heat the oil and butter in a frying pan. Drain the chops and dredge them in the seasoned flour, lightly coating both sides. Seal them in the frying pan, browning them slightly. Strain the marinade liquid into a bowl. Wash and grease the baking dish. Layer the sliced apple on the bottom and place the chops on top. Add the onion from the marinade to the fat in the frying pan. Cook until soft and stir in the remainder of the seasoned flour. Allow it to brown, stirring constantly, then gradually add the liquid from the marinade and the stock. Stir in the honey and the French mustard, bring to the boil and pour over the chops. Cover with foil and cook in a preheated oven, 350°F, for 45 minutes. Serve with peas and creamed potatoes.

Ashford Castle, today a prestigious hotel, has a history dating back to the thirteenth century, when the first castle was built on the site.

Dublin Coddle

Preparation Time: 30 minutes **Cooking Time:** 1 hour **Serves:** 4

This was regarded as a Saturday night special in Dublin and was traditionally served with Guinness.

Ingredients
8oz thickly sliced bacon
1lb pork sausages
1½lbs potatoes

1lb onions
Salt and pepper to taste

Place the bacon and the sausages in a saucepan. Cover with boiling water. Return to the boil and simmer for 5 minutes. Drain off the liquid into a bowl and reserve. Peel and slice the potatoes and onions, and place them, with the meat, in a heavy saucepan or greased casserole. Cover with the stock, season with salt and pepper and cover with wax paper before putting on the lid. Either simmer on top of the stove or in a moderate oven, 350°F, for about one hour.

An Irish bar is the perfect place to enjoy the friendliness and hospitality of the Irish people.

Boiled Chicken and Parsley Sauce

Preparation Time: 15 minutes **Cooking Time:** 3 hours 15 minutes **Serves:** 4-6

Cabbage and lovely floury potatoes boiled in their jackets are an ideal accompaniment to this dish.

Ingredients
2-3oz chicken fat
1 large boiling fowl
1 onion, chopped
Salt and Pepper

1 carrot, chopped
1 turnip, chopped
1 stick celery, chopped
A bouquet garni

Parsley Sauce
¼ cup butter
½ cup plain flour
1¼ cups stock

1¼ cups milk
Cupful of chopped parsley

Put 2-3ozs of chicken fat in a large pan. Wash and dry the bird, inside and out, and season well with salt and pepper. Brown slightly in the fat, remove and add the vegetables. Turn them in the fat for a few minutes then add the bird and cover with boiling water. Add salt, pepper and bouquet garni. Bring back to the boil, skim, then cover the pot and simmer the contents slowly for about three hours or 40 minutes to the pound.

When the bird is cooked, remove it from the pot and keep hot on a serving dish. Melt the butter in a saucepan, stir in the flour and cook for a minute. Remove from heat and gradually stir in 1¼ cups of the strained chicken stock. Return to the heat and, when it has thickened, gradually add the milk and continue cooking until it boils again. Lower the heat and cook for a further 2 minutes; add parsley and season with salt and pepper. Serve separately in a gravy boat.

The beautiful Mourne Mountains rise up into the clouds in County Down.

Spiced Beef

Preparation Time: 1 week   **Cooking Time:** 6 hours

Served cold and thinly sliced, this is a great favorite in most Irish households at Christmas time. It is not difficult to prepare at home, although it does require quite a lot of time and care.

Ingredients

6lb piece of brisket,
    sirloin tip or eye of round
3 bay leaves, finely chopped
1 tsp powdered mace
6 finely ground cloves
1 tsp crushed black peppercorns
Large clove garlic made into a
    paste with salt

1 tsp allspice
2 tbsps molasses
2 heaping tbsps brown sugar
1lb cooking salt
2 tsps saltpetre

Mix all the spices and flavorings together. Place beef in a large dish and rub well all over with the mixture. Refrigerate in a covered bowl. Repeat this process every day for a week, turning the meat and rubbing in the spices which will now be mixed with the juices drawn from the meat.

Tie the meat up firmly and rub in a final tsp of ground cloves. Cover with water and simmer slowly for six hours. When cool enough to handle remove from the cooking liquid, place in a dish and cover with a weighted plate. Slice very thinly and serve.

Ireland has some wonderful golf courses, with Dublin alone having no less than nine.

Rhubarb Fool

Preparation Time: 10 minutes **Cooking Time:** 40 minutes **Serves:** 6

Ingredients
1lb rhubarb
$1/4$ cup sugar
2-3 strips of lemon rind

$1^{1}/_{4}$ cups whipped cream
Lemon rind and mint to decorate

Trim and scrub the rhubarb and cut into 1-inch lengths. Be careful to remove all trace of the leaves, which are poisonous. Place in a buttered, ovenproof dish with a lid. Add sugar, lemon rind and about 3 tbsps water. Cover and cook in a slow oven, 300°F, for about 40 minutes or until the rhubarb is soft. Purée in a blender or food processor and allow to cool before folding in the whipped cream. Chill before serving. Decorate with mint leaves and strips of lemon rind.

The present castle of the Butlers, Cahir, County Tipperary was built in 1142, although there has been a fortress on the site since the third century.

Apple Cake

Preparation Time: 20 minutes   **Cooking Time:** 45 minutes

Ingredients

1 tsp cinnamon
1½ cups self-rising flour
¾ cup butter or margarine
¾ cup superfine sugar

3 eggs
2 tbsps milk
2-3 eating apples, peeled, cored
    and thinly sliced

Add the cinnamon to the flour and sift into a bowl. Cream butter and sugar until light and soft. Beat in one egg then add a tbsp of the flour and beat in another egg. Repeat this once more then fold in two thirds of the remaining flour. Stir in the milk then fold in the last of the flour. Grease either a lasagne dish or a roasting pan approx. 11x8½ inches. Spread half the batter in the bottom, distribute the apple slices over it and cover with the rest of the batter. Bake in the oven at 350°F for 15 minutes and reduce heat to 325°F. Continue baking for 30 minutes until golden brown and firm to the touch.

The railway line runs alongside the deserted beach at Downhill Strand.

Raspberry Soufflé

Preparation Time: 1 hour   **Serves:** 6

Because of the mild climate, Irish gardens produce bumper crops of raspberries. Raspberry Soufflé is a tasty way of using them.

Ingredients

1lb raspberries (frozen raspberries, thawed, can be used)
1/4 cup confectioner's sugar
1 envelope gelatin

4 eggs, separated
1/2 cup superfine sugar
1 1/4 cups heavy cream, lightly whipped
Mint sprigs to decorate

Tie a greased sheet of wax paper round a 6-inch soufflé dish to form a collar above the rim of the dish. Reserve a few of the raspberries and sieve the rest. Fold the superfine sugar into the purée. Soften the gelatin in half a cup of cold water, then heat over a pan of hot water until it has dissolved completely. Allow it to cool a little. Whisk the egg yolks and sugar together over the hot water. Fold in the raspberry purée and the gelatin and cool. Fold in half the cream. Whisk the egg whites until stiff, and fold into the mixture with a metal spoon. Turn into the prepared soufflé dish and leave to set. When set, remove the collar carefully and decorate the soufflé with the remaining whipped cream, raspberries and mint sprigs.

Dublin's eighteenth-century heritage is reflected in many of its traditional shop fronts.

Tipsy Cake

Preparation Time: 45 minutes   **Serves:** 8

Generally known as trifle, Tipsy Cake provided a way of using up left over sponge cakes. This version is a great standby for unexpected guests as all the ingredients can be kept in the store cupboard, apart from the cream, which can be kept in the freezer.

Ingredients

14oz can fruit cocktail
1/4 cup sherry
2oz ratafia biscuits

6 trifle sponges
Raspberry jam
2oz/60g slivered almonds

Custard

2 level tbsps cornstarch
1oz vanilla sugar (or sugar
     and 1/2 tsp vanilla extract)
1 1/4 cups milk
1 tbsp sherry

1 egg
1 1/4 cups whipped cream,
     not too stiff
Few glace cherries, halved

Drain the fruit cocktail into a bowl. Measure out 1/4 of the juice and add the sherry. Crumble the ratafias, saving some for decoration. Slice the trifle sponges in half and spread them with raspberry jam. Cut each diagonally and line the bottom of a glass serving bowl with the wedges. Place half the fruit on top and sprinkle with some ratafias and slivered almonds and 1/3 of the juice and sherry mixture. Repeat this once, then cover with the final layer of sponge and add the rest of the juice.

Place the cornstarch and sugar in a small mixing bowl, mix with 2 tbsps of the milk, bring the rest of the milk to the boil. Pour it over the cornstarch mixture, stirring constantly. Return the pan to the heat and bring the custard back to the boil and simmer for 1 minute. Remove from heat and beat in the tablespoonful of sherry and the lightly beaten egg. Cool and, while luke-warm, pour over the trifle, allowing some to trickle down between the trifle and the bowl. Chill thoroughly. Before serving top with whipped cream and sprinkle with the remainder of the ratafias and almonds and a few pieces of chopped glace cherry.

Bananas with Irish Mist

Cooking Time: 10 minutes   **Serves:** 4

Ingredients
¹⁄₄ cup butter

4 bananas

4 tsps superfine sugar

4 tsps Irish Mist (whiskey liqueur)

Melt the butter in a heavy frying pan. Peel the bananas and place them whole in the pan, turning them carefully in the melted butter. Cook them over a low heat for about 3 minutes on each side until they are heated through. Place them on individual plates and keep them warm while you make the sauce. Add the superfine sugar to the remaining butter in the pan. Stir over a low heat until dissolved. Add the Irish Mist, stir well and bring the mixture to the boil. Slice the hot bananas and spoon over the sauce.

Father Matthew Memorial Church and Parliament Bridge in the city of Cork.

Almond Tart

Preparation Time: 25 minutes **Cooking Time:** 35 minutes **Serves:** 8-10

Ingredients

6oz frozen puff paste
1/2 cup butter or margarine
1/2 cup superfine sugar
2 eggs
1 cup all-purpose flour, sifted with
    1 tsp baking powder

1/2 tsp almond extract
2 1/2 tsps milk
Damson jam
1/4 cup grated almond paste (left
    uncovered in the refrigerator to
    harden before grating)

Take 2/3 of the puff paste, roll it out thinly and line a greased 10-inch tart plate with it, allowing a 1-inch overlap all round. Roll out the remainder of the pastry slightly thicker, cut into strips 1/2-inch wide and set aside.

Cream the slightly softened butter or margarine and sugar together. Add eggs one at a time, beating well. Before adding the second egg, beat in 1 tbsp of the sifted flour. Mix the almond extract with the milk, add to the mixture then fold in the remainder of the flour.

Spread the jam on the pastry case to within 1 inch of the rim. Sprinkle the grated almond paste on top. Cover with the sponge mixture using a spatula and taking care not to disturb the filling. Make a lattice with the pastry strips over the top and crimp the edges, turning in the overlap of pastry to form a rim.

Bake in the oven at 400°F for 20 minutes, then 350°F for a further 15 minutes.

Wild deer roam free in Dublin's Phoenix Park, – one of the largest and most magnificent city parks in Europe.

Yellow Man

Preparation Time: 25 minutes

This confection has been associated for centuries with "The Ould Lammas Fair" which takes place every year at Ballycastle, County Antrim.

Ingredients

1 heaping tbsp butter
1 cup brown sugar
4 cups corn syrup

1 tsp baking powder
2 tbsps distilled white vinegar

Melt the butter in a saucepan and coat the inside of the pan with it. Add the sugar and syrup, and finally the vinegar. Stir over a low heat until the sugar and syrup have melted. Bring the mixture to the boil and simmer without stirring. Test by dropping a little into a cup of cold water to see if it sets. Add the baking powder, which will make the mixture foam up. Stir well again, pour into a greased pan and cut into squares. It may also be turned out onto a slab after the boiling process, then pulled until it becomes pale yellow in color. When it hardens it is broken into pieces with a little hammer like toffee used to be.

The National Gallery of Ireland has a large collection of old masters. A bequest by George Bernard Shaw still enables the gallery to purchase major works.

Irish Soda Bread

Preparation Time: 15 minutes   **Cooking Time:** 40-45 minutes

Soda bread is very easy to make, and it can also be bought almost anywhere in Ireland.

Ingredients

1 tsp salt
1 tsp sugar
1 heaping tsp cream of tartar
1 heaping tsp baking soda

2 cups all-purpose flour
4 cups whole-wheat flour
2 cups sour milk or fresh milk
    mixed with 1 tbsp yogurt

Add salt, sugar, cream of tartar and baking soda to the all-purpose flour. Sift into a large mixing bowl. Add whole-wheat flour and mix thoroughly with a round-ended knife, using a lifting motion to aerate the mixture. Make a well in the center and add milk, mixing until the dough leaves the sides of the bowl clean. Knead into a ball, flatten slightly and place on a greased cookie tray. Cut a cross into the top of the loaf. Brush the top with a little milk and bake in a oven, 400°F, for 40 minutes. Remove from the oven, turn loaf upside down and return to the oven for a further five minutes. The loaf is done when it sounds hollow when tapped on the base. Wrap it in a slightly dampened cloth and stand on its side to cool. Cut into quarters, slice and butter generously.

Excellent with shrimp, smoked salmon or fish paté, or at tea time with strawberry jam.

An inspiration to the poet W B Yeats, the table-top mountain of Benbulben dominates the surrounding countryside in County Sligo.

Golden Raisin Soda Bread

Preparation Time: 15 minutes   **Cooking Time:** 30 minutes

Ingredients

4 cups white, all-purpose flour
1 tsp salt
1 tsp baking soda
1 tsp cream of tartar

1 level tbsp sugar
2/3 cup golden raisins
1¼ cups sour milk or fresh milk
   with 1 tbsp yogurt mixed in

Sift flour, salt, baking soda and cream of tartar into a mixing bowl. Stir in sugar and golden raisins then add the milk, mixing to form a firm, but not too stiff, dough. Knead lightly on a floured board and form into a slightly flattened round. Cut a deep cross on the top and brush the top with milk. Place on a greased lightly floured cookie sheet and bake in center of the oven at 400°F for 25 minutes. Turn the loaf upside down on the tray and return to oven for a further five minutes. The loaf is done when it sounds hollow when tapped on the base. Wrap in a damp cloth and place on its side to cool.

Bringing in the hay in County Mayo.

Irish Coffee Cake

Preparation Time: 3-4 hours   **Cooking Time:** 35-40 minutes

Ingredients
$^1/_2$ cup butter or margarine
$^1/_2$ cup superfine sugar
2 eggs
1 cup all-purpose flour

1 tsp baking powder
2 tsps instant coffee dissolved in
   2 tbsps hot water

Syrup
$^1/_2$ cup sugar
3 tbsps Irish whiskey

$^2/_3$ cup strong coffee

Topping
$^2/_3$ cup whipping cream
1 heaping tbsp confectioners' sugar

1 tbsp Irish whiskey
Whole hazelnuts

Grease an 8-inch ring pan and coat well with flour. In a bowl, cream together the butter and sugar, then add the eggs one at a time. Sift the flour and baking powder and fold $^2/_3$ of it into the mixture. Add the 2 tbsps strong coffee. Mix well. Fold in the remainder of the flour. Place in the prepared cake pan and bake in a pre-heated oven at 350°F for 35-40 minutes. Test with a skewer and when done turn out onto a wire rack to cool.

    To make the syrup: heat sugar in coffee until dissolved, then boil rapidly for 1 minute. Remove from the heat and beat in the whiskey. Return the cooled cake to the well-washed pan and pour the syrup over it. Leave it to soak for several hours. Beat the cream with confectioners' sugar and whiskey. Turn the cake out onto a serving plate and decorate with cream and whole hazelnuts. Chill before serving.

The countryside around Ballinahinch is among the prettiest in County Galway.

Barm Brack

Preparation Time: 2-3 hours **Cooking Time:** 1 hour 10 minutes

Ingredients

$^1/_2$ tsp salt
$^1/_2$ tsp cinnamon
Pinch grated nutmeg
4 cups flour
$^1/_4$ cup softened butter
$^1/_3$ cup superfine sugar

1 cup milk, at room temperature
1 package active dry yeast
1 egg
1$^1/_4$ cups golden raisins
1 cup currants
$^1/_2$ cup cut mixed peel, chopped

Add the salt and spices to the flour and sift into a large mixing bowl. Rub in the butter. Add a tsp of the sugar and a tsp of the milk to the yeast and mix well. Add the remainder of the sugar to the flour mixture and mix in. Lightly beat the egg, add the milk, and pour this into the yeast mixture. Add this to the flour and beat very well by hand, or in a mixer fitted with a dough hook, until the batter becomes stiff and elastic. Fold in the mixed fruit and cover the bowl with lightly greased plastic wrap. Leave the bowl in a warm place for 1-2 hours, to allow the dough to rise. Divide the mixture between two greased loaf pans 8$^1/_2$x4$^1/_2$-inch, or two 7-inch cake pans. Cover again and allow to rise for half an hour. Bake for one hour in center of oven at 375°F. Dissolve a tbsp of sugar in a quarter cup of hot water and brush over brack, return it to the oven for five minutes with the heat turned off. Turn out onto a rack to cool. Slice and butter.

Gosford Castle in County Armagh was built in the Norman style for the second Earl of Gosford, Archibald Achison.

Guinness Cake

Preparation Time: 1 hour 30 minutes-2 hours **Cooking Time:** 2 hours

Ingredients
1 cup butter or margarine
1 cup brown sugar
1¼ cups Guinness ale
1½ cups raisins
1½ cups currants
1½ cups golden raisins
¾ cup mixed peel, chopped
5 cups all-purpose flour
1 tsp mixed spice
1 tsp nutmeg
½ tsp baking soda
3 eggs

Grease and line a 9-inch cake pan with greased baking parchment. Place the butter, sugar and the Guinness in a saucepan and bring slowly to the boil, stirring constantly until the sugar and butter have melted. Mix in the dried fruit and peel and bring the mixture back to the boil. Simmer for 5 minutes. Remove from the heat and cool thoroughly. Sift the flour, spices and baking soda into a large mixing bowl. Stir in the cooled fruit mixture and beaten eggs. Turn into the cake pan and bake in center of a pre-heated oven, 325°F for 2 hours. Test with a skewer. When done, cool in the pan before turning out.

The fishing port of Dingle, like almost every town in Ireland, has a wealth of pubs serving that much-loved ale – Guinness.

Recipes Compiled by Helen Walsh
Photographed by Peter Barry
Recipes Styled by Helen Burdett
Designed by Janet Barrance
Jacket Design by Justine Davies
Edited by Jillian Stewart